Yvo

God Bless

Pastor

Yvonia

SYSTEM FAILURE:
REMEDY FOR A BROKEN SYSTEM

By Douglas Gunby

SYSTEM FAILURE:
REMEDY FOR A BROKEN SYSTEM
By Douglas Gunby © 2006
www.dgunby.com

ISBN # 1-4276-1075-4

Published by Douglas Gunby
P.O. Box 1286
Decatur, GA.30031

Unless designated otherwise, scripture quotations are from the King James Version of the Bible.

Dedication

I would love to dedicate to people in my life who have helped direct me toward the purpose of God for my life in His desired time. **Kelley** and **Lee Thompson**, *thanks for always keeping me close.* **Jackie (Rodney)** and **Jaylyn**, *thanks for allowing God to use you in my life to know that I heard from Him at a young age, and never to forget to lean on Him for everything.* **Deshon "BIG DOG"** *thanks for being patient with me as I learned to raise you and relive my teen years without my father through your eyes.* **Tiffanni "Erin"**, *thanks for settling daddy down and becoming a greater inspiration for me to make sure that you, Deshon, Jaylyn, and Momi will always be taken care of.* **Momi**, *we have come from a long way, and still have a ways to go. I am proud of where we've been, the good, the bad & and the ugly. I'm glad we decided to stick it out.* I can't forget **Mrs. V. Echols**; *thanks for letting me get on your last nerve. To* **my Green Pastures Family**, *"I Love You!!!!"*

To my mother, **Collette "Lady" Gunby**, *you and dad gave Kelley and me a legacy that most would only dream of. Thank you for knowing things about me that I couldn't verbalize. You're the best!* Last, and certainly not least, I dedicate this book to the memory of the late **Ronald Earl Gunby**. *In twelve years, you gave me enough memories to last a life-time. I love you dad, and I miss you. It's ironic, the older that I get, I look, act and even sound like you. You were the greatest dad who ever lived! If it were not for the life lessons I received from you and "Lady", I don't know where I'd be.* **Thanks...**

Table of Contents

Foreword

Bishop Eddie L. Long

 God reminds us in His Word that He will raise up young men of vision, with prophetic insight, a message of righteousness, an understanding of His Word, and an anointing to overcome the kingdom of darkness (see Joel 2:28; Amos 2:11; 1 John 2:13-14). I truly believe that this book has been written by a young man that God is producing to speak life and destiny into this generation so that they can overthrow Satan's reign on this earth. I believe these pages are filled with the kind of wisdom and insight that will help men to turn their hearts back to their children and train future generations to turn their hearts back to their parents, thus eliminating the curse we are living under. (Malachi 4:6)

Every once in a while, God will place someone special in your path that you can feel, because they are saying what you are saying and going where you are going. I have been acquainted with many talented people, and I know plenty of spiritual people, but few are like Douglas Gunby. As he shares his life, his triumphs and defeats, the anointing seeps out of the broken and cracked places in his life. Through his story, parents can find hope and encouragement. Douglas shows that, though his parents were not perfect and though his life was not without pain and challenges, God is faithful to parents who have dedicated their children to God. Moreover, Douglas gives practical advice to parents as to how to speak life into, communicate with, pray with, and nurture their children. I pray that as you read these pages, the Holy Spirit would challenge you to become a man and/or woman of God, who through His principles and direction would prepare his or her children to be leaders and to take over for the kingdom of God in this next millennium.

I am so convinced that Douglas Gunby is a gift to the body of Christ, that I embrace him as a spiritual son. He is one who boldly proclaims the truth that the Church needs to hear in a way that it can digest it. I fully endorse this book for every parent, youth minister, and young person who wants to make a difference for the kingdom of God by preparing young people to be launched into their eternal destiny. I pray that as you read this book, the Holy Spirit would speak to your heart and mind, revealing to you His awesome plan for our youth and young at heart. Thank you, son, for sharing what God has laid on your heart. I am proud to have you as a son and co-laborer for Christ in His Kingdom.

Bishop Eddie L. Long, D.D., D.H.L.
Senior Pastor
New Birth Missionary Baptist Church
6400 Woodrow Rd.
Lithonia, Ga. 30038

1

The First Family

The world's system has failed us. It has taught us a lesson, through a curriculum of cruelty and injustice, that there is no safe place for man to belong in its merciless grasp. Its teachers have proven themselves to be unprepared and unconcerned with the retention of the material by its students.

The world's system was designed to put unnecessary stress on man, which causes him to feel that if he does not perform to an expected level, he is a failure. As a result of some poor decision-making skills, the man is snatched from his home, family, and way of life, only to be grouped with more broken individuals who have been secluded like animals. As a result of the flaws of this system, women have been forced to leave the prospects of remaining virtuous and the possibilities that it possesses, to achieve lucrative, ill-gotten gains. These barbaric chains of events rarely result in the man or woman returning home to function fully in their original capacity as a husband, wife, father, or mother. We must do something to change this corrupt system and protect our way of life.

In the process of disseminating information provided by this broken system, we find that the original message has been changed. As a child, I recall a game we used to play when a person would whisper a phrase shared with them to the next individual. Somewhere down the line, the information initially given was not properly communicated. With the addition of more people and the progression of the game, we waited patiently to hear whether or not the message was transferred correctly. Without fail, each time the original message had been altered; whether it was one or two words, or the entire passage, something changed. As the evidence of error became more apparent, the rules of the game dictated that the participants go back and identify the person(s) not responsible enough to listen carefully or pass the phrase properly. We often started the game over and over again to find the same results with different phrases.

By researching history, I have become a believer that the world's system has failed us by not correctly communicating the details of the original message throughout generations. We must stop playing this system's twisted game as soon as possible and put our ear back to the mouth of the Creator of the original message before another generation is deceived with misleading information.

Somewhere in the passage of time, not only did the message change, but also the system itself had been transformed. It is with great purpose, I begin this chapter with the strong statement that "The world's system has failed us." It has failed us, because a flaw was built into the inner workings of its design. Undoubtedly, there are many who would argue that a person, or a group of persons, has made a personal life vendetta to devastate another's culture or existence while here on earth.

Some may consider me naïve based on my previous statement. Believe me, I know there are those who learn to push all of the buttons that get us worked up, but there is a bigger picture. The picture that no matter which way you look at it contains more details than can be observed by the naked eye. I pose to you this question in hopes of giving you an opportunity to see another point of view. Who is the Creator of such artwork? My personal research has taught me that there are in fact two portraits that have been mastered. However, one is the original and the other, a counterfeit. The next question I inquire of you pushes you to delve deeper into your thought process.

If by reading this book, I am able to prove that there is a counterfeiter, then ask yourself, "What does the original look like, who created it, and where is it now?"

The Original Masterpiece

As a Christian, I believe in the Holy Bible (The Word of God). I have an understanding that before any information was passed down or distorted, there was an original masterpiece that for your sake, the reader, I affectionately call, "The First Family." They experienced no worries, no problems, no bills . . . nothing but peaceful serenity in the presence of God. Everything they saw was set up to benefit them. So, God created man in His image.

> *And the Lord God formed man of the dust of*
> *the ground, and breathed into his nostrils the*
> *breath of life; and man became a living soul.*
> *– Genesis 2:7*

This passage of Scripture always amazes me because for five days God spoke everything into existence. He processed thoughts, and as soon as it breeched the opening of His mouth, His thoughts became reality.

However, on the sixth day, He stopped talking and began touching. What did God touch? He touched His spoken Word. God cultivated the land to create man. I have heard it preached on more than one occasion, man came from the dust, and there was nothing wrong with that. As a matter of fact, there was nothing wrong in heaven or on earth because God said that everything to this point was good. I view God as a perfectionist who carefully paid attention to every minor detail. In the process of producing man, the Creator began to move a special component found in the earth—dirt. I know it doesn't sound spectacular, but that is what God chose to use.

Amazingly enough, everything that man needed to be self-sustained was built in since his creation. Now, God could have spoken life into man, and His Word alone would have been enough for man to live. In the sixth verse, we find that before God formed man from the dust of the ground, a mist came from the earth, which watered the face of the ground. A potter cannot form any vessel he makes without water. In the body of Christ, we relate water in every instance to the Word of God. Now knowing this new piece of information, let's look at this objectively. In the beginning, God spoke the earth into fruition. Later, we find that he stopped speaking His creations into existence to touch his final masterpiece. More important, before He began to work on this masterpiece, He caused water (the Word) to come from His previous creation to help mold and shape this final design. So, water, also known as the Word of God, was a major ingredient in the formation of man. Ironically, science has proven that our bodies are made up of 70%-75% water, but God did not stop there.

There lies man, a pile of moistened dirt touched by God. Yet, God went a step further. The Scripture said that He breathed into his nostrils the breath of life. I have been given a wonderful imagination. I can't see God as this dominating figure standing over the lifeless body of man and blowing authoritatively down on him causing his life to come into being. I see God as a compassionate Creator breathing new life into the lifeless body of man; making all of his body parts, including organs, muscles, tissues, and blood cells work in sequence with the heartbeat that God started when He breathed Himself into him. And man became a living soul, but God didn't stop there. He took the man, and put him into the Garden of Eden to dress and to keep the garden structured per the specifications of God.

God commanded man, giving him a new set of responsibilities, saying that he may consume of the fruit of every tree in the garden with one exception. The exception to the rule was that man should refrain from eating the fruit from the tree of the knowledge of good and evil, which was in the midst of the garden. He was warned that if he ate of the fruit from this particular tree, that he would suffer a consequence that no other creation of God ever experienced—death. As long as he steered clear of the temptation of this particular tree, he would not face that penalty. I imagine that this tree was tantalizingly stocked with fruit that was appealing to the eye, but carried under the bark and its vines a guaranteed path to death. Ultimately, God did create man as a perfect being, but refused to give him knowledge.

> The secret things belong unto the Lord our
> God: but those things which are revealed
> belong unto us and to our children forever,
> that we may do all the words of this law.
> —Deuteronomy 29:29

God withheld knowledge from man, not because He felt threatened by man's existence, nor because He did not want man to know as much as He did. Today's parent may withhold information that could prove harmful for his or her child in order to maintain that child's innocence. God did the same for man. More important, God withheld knowledge from man because His creation was designed without the flaw of failure, but God did equip man with the option of free will.

We were not outfitted to carry evil in our systems. Evil was nowhere near the original blueprint for our lives. As a matter of fact, God did not want man to be distracted. He knew that just the sight of this tree had the possibility to tempt man, which could cause him to stray.

> It is not good that the man should be alone;
> I will make him a help meet for him.
> —Genesis 2:18

Here we find the first mention of anything in this perfect place that was not good. I don't mean that God created something that was not good. I am saying, however, that he recognized the free will He placed in man, which caused man to become fascinated with forbidden things. This verse of Scripture states, "It is not good that man be alone . . ." One definition for the word alone is *unaided,* which also means without help. I am intrigued that after God spoke to man about the tree of knowledge of good and evil, He recognized that man could possibly be interested in partaking of the forbidden fruit this tree produced.

God wanted to remove all stumbling blocks from man's way. He said that it is not good that man be unaided (without help). God, in my opinion, took more of a personal interest in man. He kept an eye out to see that man was not swayed in any way, shape, or form by the only obstacle capable enough to make him fall. There was something God desired to add to the man, and in doing so, saw fit to take embedded materials from man to get the job done. God's purpose was to leave the man whole in his full potential while extracting and creating another whole being from the man; this we later recognize as the woman.

The Finishing Touch To Perfection

> And the Lord God caused a deep sleep to fall
> upon Adam, and he slept: and he took one of
> his ribs, and closed up the flesh instead thereof;
> And the rib, which the Lord God had taken
> from man, made he a woman, and brought her
> unto the man. –Genesis 2:21:22

When it came to creating the woman, there was still an air of mystery because man was sedated while she was being created. Adam lay in a similar position when God formed and breathed life into him. This time, instead of putting life into Adam, God removed new life from Adam, and it did not kill him. God had purpose for taking this life out of Adam. God took the woman out of man. This means that man has no feminine tendencies left in him because they were removed. Prior to God causing this sleep to fall upon Adam, he was responsible for all details of the garden, naming the animals, maintaining the landscape and everything that he saw. God removed the woman out of man, at the same time removing the ability to handle all the details of the garden alone. The woman was brought in as an equal sharer of the responsibilities God gave Adam. God did something special with the woman that man will never fully understand, because the details of God's handiwork in her were hidden from him.

When Adam was awakened from his sleep, he was not aware of what he would behold. However, God returned to Adam and presented the finishing touch of perfection to His original masterpiece. He gave Adam his very own woman, not to abuse or dominate, but to share in the abundance of God's provision. Every beast of the field and fowl of the air were duplicated after their own kind. Now, God brought to Adam his woman, and she was appealing in every way. Man is driven by vision. This woman was so stunning that Adam, the one who responsibly named everything else, claimed her by stating, "This is now bone of my bones, and flesh of my flesh: she shall be called Woman, because she was taken out of Man" (Genesis 2:23). This woman was so amazing that God did not have to worry about Adam being tempted by the tree of knowledge of good and evil anymore. Adam had the woman and the woman had her man.

He Came To Change The System

The woman was brought from the inner workings of the man to be a compliment to him. She now stands by his side to assist him in carrying out the intricate details given to him by God. Because of her position given in the garden, it has become customary at weddings that we often say, "One can put a thousand to flight, and two can put ten thousand to flight. What God has joined together, let no man put asunder." This is often spoken to signify the power in the unity of man and woman over the Enemy. Who is the Enemy?

> Now the serpent was more subtle than any beast
> of the field which the Lord God had made. And
> he said unto the woman, Yea, hath God said, ye
> shall not eat of every tree of the garden?
> — Genesis 3:1

This Enemy was obviously someone who wanted to get back at God. He would have to find a way to make God pay for ousting him and his host followers from heaven. In my opinion, the Enemy paid particularly close attention to the great detail that God put into man. He looked like God, but the Enemy learned from personal experience that God would not allow another creation in a position to attempt what he, Satan, had failed to do. So, the Enemy came in the form of a serpent. This particular animal has the ability to blend into its surroundings. Subtle and sneaky are the characteristics given to this particular beast.

He obviously realized that Adam was too enamored by the woman to be tempted by the lure of the tree of the knowledge of good and evil, so the serpent went after the woman. His aim was to get man to fall, and create uproar in heaven in hopes of exalting himself above God. So he engaged himself in conversation with this individual, other than God, who held Adam's focus.

The serpent approached the woman with some of the same words that God used with Adam in his original commandment concerning the tree of the knowledge of good and evil. He asked her, "Did God really say that you can't eat from every tree in the garden?"

> And the woman said unto the serpent, we may eat of the fruit of the trees of the garden: But of the fruit of the tree which is in the midst of the garden, God hath said, ye shall not eat of it, neither shall ye touch it, lest ye die.
> – Genesis 3:2, 3

The Enemy knows deep down that we know the truth. As a matter of fact, he's banking on that. He's betting against the possibility that you will hold to what you have come to know as the truth, and see things with a new perspective. He comes to us in many different situations, saying things that almost mimic God. He formulates his words to us with distorted undertones, which by the time they surface cause us to go back and question God's authority in our lives. The Enemy brings you the information that God originally planned to protect you from in a neat little package as if to say, "This is what God was worried you would find out about."

When You Leave The Glory

Let's take a moment to look at this enemy. The serpent was in fact the Devil in the form or likeness of a serpent. With his polished tongue, he managed to transfer seeds of his perverted thoughts provocatively to the woman. He comforted her by suggesting that eating from this tree wouldn't really cause death, but the tree possessed information that God was keeping from her. In fact, the day that she ate the fruit, it opened her eyes to see things with sight comparable to God.

Through the deception of sin, the man and woman came to possess the ability to know the difference between good and evil. Man was surrounded in the haven of everything that was good. The Enemy knew that man was inexperienced about anything that appeared evil. So the serpent presented evil in a package comparable to good, but cloaked in mystery. The Enemy approached the woman recognizing that she was superb in handling the details of the responsibilities she shared in the garden. She was invited to try her hand at what was previously introduced as forbidden.

> And when the woman saw that the tree was good for food, and that it was pleasant to the eyes, and a tree to be desired to make one wise, she took of the fruit thereof, and did eat, and gave also unto her husband with her; and he did eat. –Genesis 3:6

Something that captures a woman's attention is different from the things that capture a man's attention. God designed it that way. Daily opportunities to partake of the tree of the knowledge of good and evil were presented to Adam and Eve every time they passed the vicinity of this tree.

I believe that God, prior to taking the woman from man, took note that Adam, in particular, was sight sensitive. This means that he paid more attention to what God placed in front of him. Adam, like most men, was a visionary.

Eve differed from Adam in that she too saw the tree, but she looked at it for the possibilities it possessed. She saw that the tree was a source of food, pleasing to the eye, but an underlying thought soon surfaced. It became obvious that the woman entertained her previous communication with the serpent. She saw, once it had been communicated to her, that this particular tree could make her wise. Why did she give the tree any thought at all? The serpent observed that Adam was too taken by the woman's outward appearance to be tempted by the lure of the tree, so the serpent approached the woman with what he, through studying her, learned she enjoyed— communication. He talked to the woman and made her comfortable with what she knew to be wrong, and once she was content, Adam too was ". . . eating out of the palm of her hand." At that moment, they realized what they had done was wrong. As soon as they ate from the tree, they saw the nakedness of their bodies as evil. Although God created them, they attempted to cover their bodies.

> And they heard the voice of the Lord God
> walking in the garden in the cool of the day
> – Genesis 3:8a

I am at a loss for words when I read this particular passage of Scripture because Adam and Eve sought a hiding place from the only refuge with whom they'd had a relationship—God. Sin had taken up residence in the heart of God's original masterpieces. Adam and Eve hid themselves from the presence of the Lord among the trees in the garden.

In retrospect, I've wondered how Adam, the first man to walk and talk with God in a face-to-face atmosphere, could forget God's commandment. Although they hid from the glory of God, Adam and

18

Eve were still in His presence. When the serpent approached the woman, God was there. When Eve contemplated partaking of the fruit of this tree, God was there. When Adam, so enchanted by the beauty of his wife, failed to reiterate the commandment given to him while his wife was being convinced to accept the outlawed fruit, God was there. What made Adam and Eve think that by hiding in the trees, God would not be able to find them?

Adam and Eve had simply sinned. They had been exposed to sin, and it caused them to forget the goodness God initially showed. God began looking for the man. Why? The responsibility of everything that happened in the garden rested on his shoulders. God knew that something was different in the garden.

And Her Seed

The Lord called to Adam and asked, "Where are you?" In fact, He was saying, "Adam, where were you when the instructions I gave you needed to be followed?" The Artist walked into the gallery that housed His original masterpiece, only to find an obvious counterfeit. The Lord began to speak, but He found Adam hiding, not walking freely or taking dominion over anything in God's creation.

Adam cowered behind a tree with his wife, and with a ready excuse. He told God that when he heard the sound of His voice in the garden, his first instinct was to hide in hopes of not being seen in an uncovered manner. Previously, they were naked and not ashamed. Now, they saw their nakedness as humiliating. Sin caused drastic changes in the lives of man and woman, and in the Garden of Eden.

God asked specific information of the man, "Who told you that you were naked?" Also, He asked, "Have you eaten from the tree which I commanded that you should not eat?"

Instead of taking responsibility for his own action, Adam told God that it was the woman that he was given that offered him fruit, and he ate it. In other words, I was so focused on this woman's beauty that I didn't even recognize the tree from which the fruit came. The blame had been shifted and now God asked the woman, "What is this that you have done?" She instantly blamed the serpent saying that the serpent made her believe that evil was an ingredient found only in this particular fruit, and that God was keeping them from finding out its capabilities.

The Lord saw no more need for blame shifting and cursed the serpent. He told this creature that he would no longer maneuver as he had before or during the time of deception. The serpent was sentenced the worst curse above all other animals, including limited mobility, and a constant regimen of dust. More important, The Lord spoke of a natural hatred between the woman and the serpent, between its seed and her seed for generations to come.

2

When I Was Your Age…

Do we ever outgrow the desire to play with toys? Let's take time to probe the depth of this question. Whether we are young in age or young at heart, we will always have our toys. Girls and boys grow in stature to be women and men, and the obvious change that takes place in our lives seems physical. Our Tonka trucks and Barbie dolls blossom into life-size vehicles and gala affairs.

Men run up and down basketball courts and football fields, with great aspirations of one day receiving an enormous paycheck for playing childhood games. Women have been trained to associate the fantasy world of Ken and Barbie with reality, and try to echo the illusion. We have put down what society acknowledges as toys, only to pick up socially accepted objects of affection.

The older I got, the less likely I would have the same attractions to the toys I grew up with. I maintained a fondness for those toys, but at this stage in life, I don't rush home to get on the floor to play with them. As a matter of fact, I have gotten rid of some of them and my mother kept the rest in storage for my children.

However, age has little bearing on our being classified as men and women. Look around you, there are many examples of people who are yet unfulfilled because they have not put away childhood issues. Growth in a person is classified by responsibility, and not by age alone. A person, for the most part, is introduced to responsibility by choice or by circumstance. Whether they decide to accept the position of responsibility is left to the individual.

There were certain situations in my life when people looked at me and said, "He acts mature for his age." On the other hand, I recall being told that I was too old to act so childish. My point is simple; relationships fall apart because individuals tend to focus on what is important to them. The main reason behind this somewhat selfish point of view is that people become comfortable and refuse to see the need for change. It is very difficult to be open to other creative ideas from those who we are in a relationship with. In our human frailty, we close up and build walls, which place the blame on the other party, and we do not take time to look at ourselves.

The statement, "When I was a child," in a familiar passage of Scripture is powerful. It commands attention toward a person who has had a mind transformation and who focuses on handling their responsibilities.

I once heard a comedian on his stand-up segment make fun of a serious problem in today's society. He pointed out the subject of things we look to get extra credit for doing. Specifically, he pointed out that men look for acknowledgement for things like, "taking care of their kids." His outraged response was, "You're supposed to take care of your kids!"

Men aren't the same today as they were at an earlier time. The system in which we now live has castrated men from having a desire to take part in the lives of their own flesh and blood. Men have degenerated from being the valiant family man, to running the streets, now being on the DL (down low). How did we get here? Not all men fit in the last two categories I mentioned. There are still valiant men on this earth whose focus is to provide and speak into the lives of their families.

I personally reflect on the good times my family had together while I was growing up. My father, although paralyzed from the waist down in a wheelchair, ventured outside to play basketball with me, took me fishing, and taught me the basics of manhood. I didn't learn everything at that point, nor did I get everything right later in life. But, as I grew, I reflected on his teachings, which helped mold and shape me into the direction of manhood before the age of twelve.

My mother took the opportunity to leave her job when I was in second grade to work full time in the ministry, which was based in our home. She made this giant leap of faith to ensure that our house was also a home. After the death of my father, my mom taught me what it was like to be a man from the legacy my dad left with her. My sister and I grew up side by side with our parents while they worked for the ministry.

My heart goes out to the families in the world today, specifically here in America. Almost 75 percent of America's homes are fatherless. Even more amazing, half of the remaining 25 percent of America's homes have fathers in them, but he does not communicate effectively with the inhabitants of his home. There is no such thing as perfect. I have grown to understand that everybody comes from a broken home. The stereotypical broken home has crossed the lines of race and income. We've gone from two-parent homes to majority single-parent homes mainly through deaths, divorce, or lack of communication. We are even embarking upon the unstable foundation of same-sex marriage with which these abnormal families are daily gaining the rights to adopt other broken youth to show them a *new perspective*. The man, in this new system, is slowly being taken out of the picture. And it is my belief that men are accepting this new position because they do not understand how vital they really are to their families. The reason they accept it is because the information has been altered.

The key contributor to an individual's success is the support received from parents, and fathers in particular. I feel fortunate that Kelley and

I had parents who communicated with us so intently that when circumstances arose, we excelled by leaps and bounds. They informed us that we would go through things to learn lessons, but in the end, we would conquer the problem.

After our father passed, I faced a number of childhood and adult-related issues. I faced some of the challenges with my mother's help, but mostly alone. There were inward battles, great and small. I tried to conquer them on my own, but found this phrase to be true: "You win some and you lose some." The battles my mom helped me face were difficult, but easy to overcome. She taught me respect for other people, and definitely reinforced many other things she and my father previously introduced. She was, and still is, an instrument that cuts me open and stitches me up again and again. I speak about my mother affectionately because I love her dearly. She has helped me find resolutions to my issues through this one phrase that seemed to be repeated way too many times: "When I was your age . . ."

People today face many challenges and have many opportunities to overcome breathtaking obstacles in life. Throughout life, we learn through growth and maturity, to discern the truth as it relates to us. I recall when my parents instructed me in a direction that was to prove better for me than my own thoughts, and I reluctantly gravitated toward their words. I did so mainly because I saw that my ideas were not working at all the way I planned.

My parents trained us to listen to and follow wisdom. Their words challenged my limited beliefs, and that truly intrigued me. All of my life, my mother reminded me that throughout the duration of her pregnancy with me, she dedicated my life to the Lord to be used by Him. She never permitted me to forget the words of her promise. More important, every time I approached the brink of trouble, her words would snatch me back into the reality that I have a greater purpose on this earth. Her words to me were, "Only what you do for Christ will last."

What Influences You?

Influence is one reason that so many youth are being drawn away through devices such as music, sex, drugs, and finances. People have not accepted the reality that there is an enemy who makes daily attempts to infiltrate and destroy their lives. Likewise, there are very few influential individuals to remind these people that their lives have both destiny and purpose.

As an example, music has taken the most influential forefront in the mainstream of life. It has become more prevalent in homes, schools, and in the lives of people everywhere through all major mediums. A person no longer goes to the club to hear the latest musical hits. They just turn on the radio, television, or go to the movies. Music is everywhere. The lyrics of songs feed into who a person thinks he or she should be. The individual finds a way to relate to those words and sometimes they take on the persona of a particular song.

When I think back, I was a huge West Coast Rap fan. I have been in church all my life, but like most people, I began searching for a new identity. In particular, the West Coast gangster mentality appealed to something deep within me. I was not violent by a long shot. In all actuality, I was in the church seven days a week. That genre of music appealed to my sin nature, and to a nature that I later found was present in my father that, in time, attached itself to my life. I found myself fighting as a youth, and even as an adult, anxious for anyone to cross a line I'd drawn in the sand. In retrospect, I recall my mom telling me that the very same sin nature put my father in a wheelchair. That is a very sobering thought for me. As a result, I have found outlets such as motorcycles, basketball, and most recently, golf, which relieve great stress from me.

I have asked young people specifically about the music they listen to. I have taken such an interest in their future that I listen to the music with them to help disseminate the information they are putting into their systems.

Amazingly, we have wonderful conversations because I am not just another adult telling them not to listen to it, but I'm showing them the hidden messages in the music. Ironically, the more you tell a young person not to participate in an event that may prove a danger for them, the more they become willing to find ways to indulge themselves in that very thing.

Vulgar music is not the disease or the problem. It is simply a symptom of the problem. Let's get to the heart of the problem. In my experience, I find that the problem is the search for significance, which takes me back to the home, and the covering or lack thereof. A scary recurrence for me is to see mothers, fathers, and children, even grandparents, walking around singing songs like, "To the window, to the wall!" Most of today's popular music asserts using women as illicit sex toys as a means of making money.

The song "Tip Drill" stirred a great deal of controversy because the content of the video was ridiculous. It portrayed women in lewd positions in saunas, backyards, and draped over one another. As a father, I am scared for my daughter and son in this society. Sadly, it is not just in rap music that we've lost direction. Our directions have been misconstrued because, once again, the message has been altered. The music that is being produced promotes a false need for love and approval from sources that don't love back. The lyrics of today's songs have become vulgar, degrading, and filled with ideas of grandeur.

There is a promise that before the second arrival of Christ, there will be a spiritual awakening in the parents and their children. There will be oneness where there was no unity, and it's all going to point back to God. The wayward child will return and accept the knowledge that was previously rejected. We smile on parents for successfully raising their children by social standards. Most times, we honor parents after the child has become someone important, but what about encouraging the parent of that child whose future does not appear to be so bright. **A confident person has a greater opportunity to succeed**.

My father, the late Ronald E. Gunby, and my mother, Collette L. Gunby, raised me into completeness. Many people have tried to take credit for the person I have become, but when the ending acknowledgements roll on my life, their names will be visible, and in bold print! Although my father died on January 19, 1986, he left a legacy on paper with the trust in God that his family would persistently pursue the specified plans. Due to my parents somewhat difficult, but all-the-time loving relationship, they have raised two of the world's most influential people. How did my mom accomplish raising respectable children without a physical man in the house? While busy in ministry, and business, she found time to be with us. It was in those times she was guided and strengthened in her inner man. Society said it could not be done, but God said it must be done.

Looking back, I don't see how else my mother could have survived, except that she spent time with God. There were many nights I heard my mother praying to God about successfully bringing her children to Him; allowing at the same time, for Him to be glorified. Many times, my mother talked to me about my life, and I'm sure there were instances when she may not have had a clue how to help me. But experience with my father provided insight as to what was going on with me. She simply, but firmly, spoke words that would bring calm to my situation. Most of the time, words were not enough. It was more important that she show me, so I received many butt-whippings as motivation. My parents experienced many things that afforded me the opportunity to look back on and learn from. Things I do even now remind my mother of things my father did when he was my age.

The Pickle Jar

I received an interesting, anonymous story by e-mail titled "The Pickle Jar" that talks about a father's love for his child and how significant his child's future was to him.

The pickle jar, as far back as I can remember, sat on the floor beside the dresser in my parents' bedroom. When he got ready for bed, Dad would empty his pockets and toss his coins into the jar. As a small boy I was always fascinated at the sounds the coins made as they were dropped into the jar. They landed with a merry jingle when the jar was almost empty. Then the tones gradually muted to a dull thud as the jar was filled. I used to squat on the floor in front of the jar and admire the copper and silver circles that glinted like a pirate's treasure when the sun poured through the bedroom window. When the jar was filled, Dad would sit at the kitchen table and roll the coins before taking them to the bank. Taking the coins to the bank was always a big production. Stacked neatly in a small cardboard box, the coins were placed between Dad and me on the seat of his old truck.

Each and every time, as we drove to the bank, Dad would look at me hopefully. "Those coins are going to keep you out of the textile mill, son. You're going to do better than me. This old mill town's not going to hold you back." Also, each and every time, as he slid the box of rolled coins across the counter at the bank toward the cashier, he would grin proudly.

"These are for my son's college fund. He'll never work at the mill all his life like me." We would always celebrate each deposit by stopping for an ice cream cone. I always got chocolate. Dad always got vanilla. When the clerk at the ice cream parlor handed Dad his change, he would show me the few coins nestled in his palm. "When we get home, we'll start filling the jar again." He always let me drop the first coins into the empty jar. As they

rattled around with a brief, happy jingle, we grinned at each other. "You'll get to college on pennies, nickels, dimes, and quarters," he said. "But you'll get there. I'll see to that."

The years passed, and I finished college and took a job in another town. Once, while visiting my parents, I used the phone in their bedroom, and noticed that the pickle jar was gone. It had served its purpose and had been removed.

A lump rose in my throat as I stared at the spot beside the dresser where the jar had always stood. My dad was a man of few words, and never lectured me on the values of determination, perseverance, and faith. The pickle jar had taught me all these virtues far more eloquently than the most flowery of words could have done. When I married, I told my wife Susan about the significant part the lowly pickle jar had played in my life as a boy.

In my mind, it defined, more than anything else, how much my dad had loved me. No matter how rough things got at home, Dad continued to doggedly drop his coins into the jar. Even the summer when Dad got laid off from the mill, and Mama had to serve dried beans several times a week, not a single dime was taken from the jar. To the contrary, as Dad looked across the table at me, pouring catsup over my beans to make them more palatable, he became more determined than ever to make a way out for me. "When you finish college, son," he told me, his eyes glistening, "You'll never have to eat beans again...unless you want to."

The first Christmas after our daughter Jessica was born; we spent the holiday with my parents. After dinner, Mom and Dad sat next to each other on the sofa, taking turns cuddling their first grandchild. Jessica began to whimper softly, and Susan took her from Dad's arms. "She probably needs to be changed," she said, carrying the baby into my parents' bedroom to diaper her. When Susan came back into the living room, there was a strange mist in her eyes. She handed Jessica back to Dad before taking my hand and leading me into the room. "Look," she said softly, her eyes directing me to a spot on the floor beside the dresser. To my amazement, there, as if it had never been removed, stood the old pickle jar, the bottom already covered with coins. I walked over to the pickle jar, dug down into my pocket, and pulled out a fistful of coins. With a gamut of emotions choking me, I dropped the coins into the jar. I looked up and saw that Dad, carrying Jessica, had slipped quietly into the room. Our eyes locked, and I knew he was feeling the same emotions I felt. Neither one of us could speak.

I pose this question to you as I end this particular chapter. *What are you willing to sacrifice to ensure the success of your children?*

3

Born With A Purpose

There was a young married couple that loved one another. They had been married for five years, and believed God for children in the near future. Their lives had begun to synchronize, and their finances had reached a level that would allow them to do greater things.

The couple soon became aware they were about to have a baby. They began to prepare all the necessary things to responsibly bring a baby safely into the world. All the scheduled doctor's appointments and instructions were followed to the letter. As the months passed, the couple discovered they were having twins. The months continued to go swiftly by, and soon it was time to deliver the babies. The expectant parents anxiously anticipated the birth of the twins. One by one, as the babies entered their new world, the father's eyes filled with tears.

In preparation for the arrival of the children, the parents pre-selected their names. The parents discovered they were having a boy and a girl. The boy would be named Today. He was extremely vibrant and alert. And the little girl was named Tomorrow. She was very quiet and peaceful. The two were always together; you would never see one without the other. Their parents raised them to respect themselves, each other, and other people as individuals. As they grew older, they never grew apart. Everything they did was done together from birth to the twelfth grade.

When they graduated, their parents gave them both puppies. The puppies, like Today and Tomorrow, were twins. The parents had also previously named the pups, and they planned to explain the significance of all names mentioned. The mother handed the puppies to the father, and he in turn, passed the pups to Today and Tomorrow. As the twins received the puppies, their father began to speak.

He said, "Your mother and I have already named the puppies. Today, your puppy is named Youth, and Tomorrow, yours is named Wisdom." The twins looked puzzled as their father continued to speak. He said, "Today, take Youth and enjoy him; learn from his frisky ways, and relish being with him."

"Tomorrow, observe Wisdom and exercise patiently with her. Learn from her as she becomes obedient to each command you give. When you visit your brother, give Youth the training that Wisdom has received. As they are further acquainted, more of their individual personalities will transfer to each other. Youth will learn from Wisdom, and Wisdom will take on the characteristics of Youth."

From that day forward, Today and Tomorrow were excited about their futures because Youth and Wisdom would play intricate roles in each of their lives. In other words, their parents directed them to the path that led to purpose.

How many times have you wondered what your purpose is while here on earth? How many people live on this earth feeling insignificant? To start, let's look at the suicide rate, divorce rate, high school dropout rate, and unemployment rate. Looking at statistics simply informs me that people are in trouble and they need help. I am not perfect, nor do I have it all together because you're reading the pages of this book. I felt as if I had a purpose, but I was not always aware of what it was. I was confused because different events in my life were designed to equip me for my purpose, but I ran from the challenges. I ran until I realized that everywhere I ended up put me in similar situations. I could not escape. I compare finding purpose to being incarcerated. Once you get locked into purpose, it follows you for the rest of your life.

I have never been physically imprisoned. I have not experienced sitting inside a six-by-nine-foot cell, waiting for my time to be released. But I do know what it is like to live a frustrated, unsatisfied life, looking for answers and barely finding any. However, I have discovered that when I locked into my purpose, I found a new freedom. I discovered a greater reason to live. I gained a new outlook on life. The reason I was never physically locked up was the fact that my mother told me, "If you get locked up, you stay locked up!" That was enough for me.

When I was initially placed into my purpose, I cried to God, asking him to release me. "How do you expect me to fill that position, Lord?" I reminded God of all the wrong things that I had done. "I'm an alcoholic, I smoke weed, I have a foul mouth, and I'm a womanizer!" "How is it that you now want me to do this?" In time, I realized I was operating in my purpose. I learned how to be free from my old habits and stay free. I wasn't clean when I came to know the Lord. Here's how it happened for me.

God alone touched my life. Some friends and I were in a hotel suite in Savannah, Georgia. We had planned an unauthorized vacation for the weekend. We were down there, drinking and smoking marijuana the whole weekend, just having a crazy party.

On Saturday night, I was over in the girls' suite watching a rerun of the Holyfield/Douglas fight. During the course of the contest, I smoked a joint and consumed an immense amount of alcohol. When Holyfield hit "Buster" Douglas, it was just as if he'd hit me. I began to slouch down in the chair, and as I descended, I caught a glimpse of a black figure coming down the stairs of the suite. The shadow moved down the stairs, and no one saw it but me. I told everyone that I'd caught a glimpse of a shadowy entity; of something evil. The moment I saw it, I gathered everyone together and went to the other suite with my boys. I gathered the other *church folks* into the guys' suite too, and my voice trembled when I tried to tell them what I saw.

"We are not supposed to be here!" I exclaimed. I was as sober then as I am right now. I just remember praying and asking God to forgive us for abusing His love. Those who were there with me assumed that I was just stoned out of my mind and sent me to bed, but God was working on me.

My name, Douglas, which means "Seeker of Light," began to take on new meaning as I searched for a way to get out of the downward spiral I was in. September 28, 1992, was the last day I ever smoked or drank alcohol in my life. God began to show me how to face life, instead of running from it. That's the very same thing an addict does—he runs from life. I was addicted to the wild life. The Enemy is attempting the very same thing with you. He is trying to throw you off your God-given course that was set before you were even born.

What was my purpose? At this particular place in my life, I was living to the full potential of my own limited expectations, but God had a better plan for me—more than I could ever imagine. It turned out that my purpose was all tied up in my past. The Enemy convinced me that self-indulgence was normal. Those particular vices—drinking, smoking weed, and womanizing—turned out to be tools I later used to help individuals who were struggling in those same areas.

Got It . . . What Next?

After my experience in Savannah, I could not go on with life as usual. I felt the tug of an unsure destiny, but I was afraid, so I resisted its pull as long as I could. I knew where I had been, but the problem was the guilt or fear of telling others the things I had done. My life was a mess, but I began to see a glimmer of hope. I had allowed many wrong influences to control my every waking thought. I was afraid of what others thought about me, and as a result, I had no voice of my own. I let alcohol speak for me when I could not speak my thoughts in public. I used alcohol as an excuse, and no matter what I said, people would just disregard my comments as, "He's drunk!"

Even as outgoing as I am, I could not address a cute young lady without a little joy juice in my system. How did I get to this point? Somehow, the information in my life's system had been altered. It reminds me of the times prior to the death of my dad. My father was very verbal about the things he believed God wanted him to share with his family. He spoke to us on many occasions: over dinner, at the park, or riding in the car. He took advantage of every opportunity to talk to us about things we later found to be true. His heart had been transformed from what I heard was a real mess to a man truly searching for the pulse of God. After his death, I began to shut down in every relationship I had. The only person who could get me to open up was my sister because I felt that she was the only person who truly understood what I was going through. Obviously, we were dealing with the same problem, and we identified with one another.

I slowly began to withdraw from society and learned to mask my fears and hurts so that others would not know the pain I was experiencing. Although I was gradually entering a maturing process, the void in my life became larger. I began experimenting with different things in an attempt to fill the cavity, but those things only caused the chasm to widen.

As a result of this gaping hole, I found myself in a comfort zone of anger and resentment. I liked being angry because it kept people at more than an arm's distance. I did not want anyone to get too close, and I purposed that no one, not even my mom, would get close to me. I tried everything in the book and those events in my life drove me further away from the original message God planned for my life.

So as my life began to come full circle, I asked God, "What next?" I was quickly reminded that everything I had gone through was not just for my edification, but I went through those things to help someone else make it out just as I did. I was not a "hellion," but I was very mischievous.

Sometimes, as individuals, we think that we are the only ones going through particular chains of events in our lives. But we later find that the very thing we went through, God used to encourage someone else. Over the course of time, and through many more experiences, I came to the place that I can share some of those experiences to help you.

The Heart of A Father

As I mature into manhood, I am learning to view women in a greater light. I sometimes ask myself the following questions. What particular course of events caused me to desire to honor and respect the gracefulness of womanhood? Was it being the only male in a single-parent home with a mother and sister who ran the family business after the death of my father? Was it giving my heart in marriage to a beautiful woman, which opened my eyes to the many strengths of a woman? I understand that women possess strength, independence, and an abundance of wisdom, and there is no doubt these strong, independent women were very instrumental in shifting my view of women.

However, none of those things stimulated my desire to know the mysterious makeup of a woman. The one particular event in my life that enhanced my viewpoint was holding my daughter in my arms moments after her arrival in April 2002. As she lay there holding my finger and firmly pressed it to her mouth, my mind's eye could see brief glimpses of her life from that moment as an infant to her preparation for marriage. My heart began to race as I saw a brief glimpse of what I would face as a father. The only sobering thought for me in those moments of panic was realizing that I was present in those scenes to help her each step of the way. This simple, yet magnificent, event set in motion a new outlook on women, and I began the journey from a man to a father.

Both men and women must transform their views of one another. Our male-dominated society depicts today's woman as a money hungry, sexual trashcan to be used in any form at a man's discretion. Even more astonishing, some women have accepted this stereotype as a reality. Turn on your television at any time during the day, and my position will easily be validated. Women have followed this dangerous path specifically for one reason. They are searching for acceptance and significance from a man; sometimes, any man. My daughter, now three years old, loves to try on pretty dresses. She will try them on for the first time, and immediately come searching for me. As she twirls around to showcase her new dress, she smiles and eagerly awaits my reaction. It does not matter how tired I may be, or what appointments I have to keep, I am compelled to respond to her call for approval and significance. Many grown women are still twirling around, waiting for the reaction of a man. Most will not admit it, but if this type of love and validation *is* received from a father, the snare of unhealthy relationships can many times be avoided.

Ladies, I want to help you. It takes a *real man* to treat you the way you deserve to be treated. It takes a *real man* to respect you. It takes a *real man* to provide for you. Last, it takes a *real man* to provide affirmation and support so that you may be able to fulfill your destiny. This does not mean that you must depend on a man for your success in life. It simply means that in order to achieve greater success, this affirmation is a key ingredient. The first man who is responsible for that is a father. In our present day, we don't have many fathers; we have babies' daddies. Those fathers are little boys still playing games with their lives and yours. A father, the *real man*, looks at a woman with the understanding that he must do everything in his power to make her life the best it can be.

There is an awesome responsibility for women to collectively change the stigma of a black cloud that hangs over their heads. How is this change going to come about? This will occur when a woman hears from a real man who is not out for what she can give him, but for the valuable information she can learn from him. Time and time again it has been said, and is still relevant today—will the *real men* please stand up? There are young men and women wandering the streets in search of their purpose, but finding no answers. I am in search of men dedicated to the cause of preserving our future. We cannot afford for you to remain silent, whether you are in the home or not. ***Open your mouth and let your heart speak!*** Our families' purpose is on a ship that is about to sail away. We must teach them, "If the ship does not come in, swim to it!" Don't let your purpose get away from you.

4

Dad is Looking For Results

There are various methods that fathers and mothers use to handle situations that involve their children. These methods differ because the makeup of a man and woman is completely opposite. My father was straight and to the point, as most men are. Whatever he said was supposed to be done, no questions asked. After his death, I went through a very turbulent time as a young person. My mom would sit down and attempt to have a simple conversation with me. Her words would strike that nerve of grief and loss, and I would blow up with anger that I didn't know I possessed, much less know how to control.

In retrospect, I somehow feel I could have adjusted to that drastic time in my life if my father had only prepared me. I could have handled issues in my life totally different if I just knew what would happen to the one man that held the most influence in my life.

I missed the family day trips to Helen, Georgia. Although we still took trips, it was not the same. Instead of a family unit handling the challenges of life, we became three broken people trying our best to bandage one another's wounds. My mom would talk to us and her words almost suffocated me, and I would shut down. I couldn't handle the change that had taken place—the death of my father.

I remember the last time I saw my father alive. It was January 17, 1986. I was outside playing with the other children whose parents worked for our church and school. I ran around the stairwell and elevator to see my dad loading his wheelchair into the backseat of our navy blue Cadillac. He was wearing a navy blue, knit collar shirt with white horizontal stripes and tan khakis. He called me over to the driver's side to give me instructions on how to act while he was away at the hospital. He said he loved me and kissed me on my lips as he'd always done.

"Yes sir," I said, "I love you too." I went back to playing. Little did I know I would never again see my dad with life in his body? For our family, Dad being in the hospital was nothing new. We went so often; we grew to have personal relationships with the staff at DeKalb General Hospital. To my sister and me, this was just another day that Dad went to the hospital. We expected to see him when the doctors said that he cooperated with them.

That Saturday morning, I had my very first basketball game, which we lost, at the Clarkston Baptist Church gymnasium. My sister's responsibility was to take care of me whenever my mom had to be at the hospital with my dad. The basketball team always went to Steak 'n Shake after each game whether we won or lost. My sister would then take me to the mall so she could shop, and I could salivate over things I couldn't afford. For some reason we never made it to see Dad at the hospital that day. On Sunday, we had church and went to dinner after the service to celebrate my parents' secretary's birthday at Pittypat's Porch in downtown Atlanta. After dinner we planned to go to the hospital to share with my dad how the service went and sneak in some food (with the nurse's knowledge, of course). But something was different this time. When we got to the floor, the nurses met us at the door of the ICU. They escorted my sister and me to a waiting room, which they had never done.

"They must be changing Daddy's hip dressing," my sister said. (He had a hole in his hip from sitting in the wheelchair.) I said okay and we waited. It was approximately six-thirty, but we never paid any attention to the time. As a matter of fact, we were using the phonebook to make prank phone calls when the door opened, and I saw my mother being helped to her feet by the doctors and nurses.

Tears slid down her face, and she said, "Your daddy died!" I vividly recall the tone of her voice. I heard a mixture of pain, uncertainty, and anger rolled into one. She walked over to embrace us, and I cried. The more I thought about it, my dad died like most men live— **ALONE**. They all have families, but oftentimes the family is not around when he needs them. No one understands that a man needs his family; people rarely recognize in today's society that the family needs the man.

I remember being escorted down a hall that seemed to stretch for miles, to the room where my dad's lifeless body lay. I stood next to his left leg and held onto his finger seeking the comfort that I cherished, but I didn't feel comforted. The next thing I remember, I was standing at the door of the Cadillac. I opened the door for my mom and sister to get in, and I stared at the moon, shaking my head. "No!" I said. The moon was the only thing I could relate to God at that moment. I felt my body begin to shiver as   tears slid down my face, and I began asking God, "Why?" All I wanted to know was, "Why did my dad have to die at this point in my life?" "Why was I left alone now?" "What would I do when I didn't know the answers to the many questions I had?"

At that point in my life, I hated God for taking my father from me. If I could just stand face to face with God, I would choke the life out of Him. After all of the wonderful things I had seen God do in my life and in the lives of others, I didn't want Him to offer me anything else. When I realized that my dad was dead, a huge piece of me died with him—a piece that I didn't realize was gone until I began writing this section of the book.

I love my mother, and in no way can I discredit the impact she made in my life, but my father and I had a bond like no other. My dad taught me many wonderful things like how to drive the family car at 75 mph on I-20 while sitting in his lap, eating oysters and crab legs, fishing, and how to be responsible for what God had graced me with. More important than any of these things my dad taught me, I look back with special fondness because he took time to teach me the game of basketball while sitting in his wheelchair.

Teaching basketball would be very difficult for the average man, but not for my dad. I watched him transfer his body out of the wheelchair and into the car, so he could move it from under the basketball goal. Then he got back out of the car to talk me through the steps of the game. Most men won't even get off the sofa to change the channel on the television.

In my eyes, my dad could do anything. I only hope to be as great a father and husband to my wife and children as he was to our family. I would like to do something different with the next three chapters that I personally have never seen done. I want to impart purpose into my wife and children and also to you describing what I believe God desires for families. My hope is that men will take the initiative to speak life into their families. When this happens, then it is my belief that sons, daughters, wives, and even babies' mamas will change.

5

My Heart Is Turned Toward You

As I began gathering my thoughts on this chapter, I was fortunate to be home watching some reruns of my favorite television shows. I caught glimpses of the Cosby Show, and it was another episode in which Denise was attempting to make yet another life decision. However, while flipping through the channels, the show that caught my attention and caused me to totally focus on its content was The Fresh Prince of Bel-Air. The show began with Will and Carlton working in the Peacock, the college hangout. Will noticed a man who had been watching him ever since he entered the restaurant. Will reluctantly, yet cautiously, approaches the gentleman to inquire why he had been watching him and is shocked by the way he is addressed.

It had been fourteen years since the last time Will, as a five-year-old, had contact with his father, Lou. Will was quickly reminded of who Lou was the moment he called him son.

The show provided different instances of contact between Will and Lou, and culminated with Uncle Phil and Lou having a man-to-man discussion about Lou's empty promises to Will, and Lou's cowardly way of backing out of his son's life again. Will was not validated by the one who was responsible for his existence, and unfortunately, he entered the room in time to hear the lame excuse Lou gave.

As a maturing young man, Will's character had been strengthened, but only to a certain extent. He, in a sense, bravely put on his game face in front of the man who had disappointed him the majority of his life. Lou slunk out   the door leaving a nineteen-year-old young man and the man that truly filled the void in his life—Uncle Phil. The two of them stood face to face. Uncle Phil allowed this young man to express his feelings, which without a doubt brought tears to Uncle Phil's eyes—and mine.

Will began to say, *"You know what, I'm going be okay. My game was weak when it came to basketball, but I managed to train myself and got better. I didn't know how to talk to girls, but through trial and error, I even got good at that. As a matter of fact, I just realized something, I trained myself in all of those things, so I am sure that I can find a fine honey, have some beautiful kids, and be a better father than he ever was to me. 'Because you know what, I don't need him!"*

That statement is a sad reality for youth all around the world. The scary part of that reality is that these symptoms didn't begin in the new millennium. They have been present for generations, and have now reached a dangerous level, which if not addressed, will alter society, and everyone will experience the irreversible effects of it. Fathers have been out of place too long, but not long enough to accept these irrefutable consequences. I am a believer that if a man takes the time to get his life in order first, then everything he is responsible for has to line up as well. My purpose in writing this particular chapter is to set in motion the rusted wheels of time that have the greatest potential to restore man to his lost dominion.

A Message to You Son
Deshon "BIG DOG" Gunby

Every morning I get out of bed, I take time to gather my thoughts for the day. They constantly travel across the various regions of my mind as the course of my day moves forward. These thoughts are so consuming that I am motivated to get out of bed without an alarm clock startling me to attention. One question that causes moments of meditation is that which involves you, son.

I often think, "What can I teach my son today that will make the path he will have to travel a lot easier?" I attempt to reflect on some of the ways that I remember my dad teaching me, and try my best to duplicate some and improve on others. It may seem that I'm not very verbal, when in reality; I am speaking loudly through my actions. My responses are not limited because of a lack of words, but they are purposefully instructional. All of your life, I have desired to teach you things that will make your life flow, as well as eliminate some of the problems that you could face later. No, I am not dying nor am I going to leave, but I am doing what I think a man should do. I am speaking into your life the things that I believe God wants me to say to you. As a matter of fact, there is not enough paper for me to pen all the information I have in my head toward you. More important, I believe it is not my job to dictate your life, but prepare you to walk out the steps of your life. I purposely made attempts to approach you with things I remember facing when I was your age. However, I made greater attempts to safely share with you some of the pitfalls that I faced. Strangely enough, I remembered how I saved myself from a few of those pitfalls, and how God Himself had to come get me from others. I never hid the fact that I used to drink alcohol to impress my buddies, and drown my sorrows in a futile attempt to find answers. I also told you that sometimes the alcohol wasn't enough to suppress some of my depression, so I turned to smoking marijuana, which caused me to feel worse. Son, anyone can tell you to stay away from drugs, but I am taking the time to tell you that drugs are really a waste of time, and you are too important for me to allow you to waste your life. Most men teach their sons to refrain from alcohol and most drugs, but allow them to partake of the strongest drug of them all—women.

Just recently, I explained to you the importance of remaining a virgin until you get married. I told you that I wished I had waited until I had gotten married before I had sex. My reason for sharing that with you was simply to let you know that as much as I love your mom, premarital sex made it hard for me to give my heart totally to the one woman I love. Over time, and with the help of God, I was able to give my heart totally to your mother, but I don't want you to face those sometimes hopeless consequences. Most men won't tell their sons, but women are one of the hardest challenges for a man to get beyond. They are more addictive than any drug on the street. One hit from a woman could leave you spellbound to the point that you would do anything for her. Son, let that one hit be from the woman you marry and spend the rest of your life with. Don't get caught up in being someone's baby's daddy. That is not the plan your mother and I have for you. I know that one day, you're going to be your own man, but if you listen to me now, you can be a better man later.

There's A Leader Within You

As a father, I am observant. It doesn't take much to make me proud; however, it does require a great deal of effort on my part for you to experience how proud I really am of you. Men are generally perceived as non-responsive, but I, with the help of your mother, am learning to show my softer side and still feel like a man. Actually, even writing this chapter to you has helped me feel manlier than I ever have before. Son, you are more important to me than I've ever had the opportunity to express. I fondly think back to the time when you were four years old. Your mother and I were dating, and we were going somewhere with my mom and sister. Everyone was having such a great time. I was driving, the ladies were talking, and you were sitting in the middle between your mom and my sister. For one reason or another, you felt the need to get my attention, and without hesitation, you said, "Daddy." At that moment, an awkward silence fell in the vehicle. Everyone looked at one another, then they looked at me, and I responded with an assured, "Yes, son." No man is sure that he will be a good man, and more important, a good father. However, at that moment I knew I was ready to be a father, and more than that, be your father.

In training you for the challenges of life, I felt the need to involve you in many facets of my life. You have been in million-dollar meetings with me. You have even signed papers as a participant in those meetings. I always wanted to involve you in anything I felt could teach you lessons that you could use later in life. I never wanted you to think   life was going to be easy, and when I approached a rough area in my life, I shared what I could with you. I have tried my best to be open and honest with you about the stresses that life will bring, but most important, I have taught you to be persistent to see those challenges through until the end. Everything has not been perfect, but together, you and I have worked through it. I find you to be a very serious young man with a secret silly side. Please, don't ever lose that. Your unique character will some day be the very thing that helps you keep your sanity.

Deshon, I love you like no other man can. Your mother and I have taken the time to invest into you the things of God. I am pleased with the returns from those investments. Continue to strive to be the individual that God called you to be. You have your own path, which is different from anyone else, even mine. Pursue your path with a passion to see the end result. The older you get, know that life will toss many challenges your way. Never be afraid to come to your mother and me so we can help you face those challenges, and then you'll become the man that God has called you to be. You are a leader. I know everybody likes to tell their children those famous words, but I really believe you are. However, I want to tell you what exactly leadership requires of you. Son, remember these five points, and you can't go wrong.

Leadership compels you to have vision and goals that bring honor to God, and helps to maintain your good name. Son, your vision consists of those wonderful ideas you have in which the end result benefits and enhances the lives of others, and it helps to sustain your life and the life of your family.

Once you have a God-honored vision, then you must gather people toward the vision that can help you achieve the necessities for that vision. Your mother and I have made great attempts to teach you how to choose your friends wisely. We have taught you to look for those individuals who are not just your friend or who associate with you when it's convenient for them. Once you establish and become comfortable in finding these types of relationships, there is another piece of information I wish to add.

You must possess the capability to motivate those that work side by side with you to make the thankless tasks of the job exciting.

Leadership instills the desire to learn, and will teach you to sense the need for change and ways to constructively bring that change about. It teaches you to prioritize your position to that of a servant, not to be trampled on, but to be the best a leader can be.

The final and most important aspect of leadership that I desire for you to learn is that you must take the time to train someone else to some day take the reigns of leadership. You test your leadership skills based on your ability to duplicate yourself in others.

Remember, all the answers to your every question are tied up in your mom and me. We are so proud of you, and we look forward to seeing the man you will become. We love you.

A Message To Daddy's Girls

There is a special bond between a father and his baby girl. However, this bond in no way diminishes the relationship of a father and son. I personally have grown to appreciate when a daughter surrenders knowledge about women that a man sometimes lacks. A daughter presents a father the opportunity to start from scratch. Little girls give fathers the opportunity to protect her from hurts and disappointments that he may have caused other women in his past. He feels the need to be accountable for making sure that his daughter does not fall for the same strategies he used on other little girls when he was growing up.

I have been blessed when it comes to children. I have a handsome son, as you can tell from the photo. I also am the proud father of two little girls. Jaylyn Williams, my God-given daughter, has been a part of my life since she was eighteen months old. For the record, this does not mean I have taken the place of her biological father, but I do have an understanding that she was placed in my life to help develop her life's purpose. I also am the father of Tiffanni Erin Gunby. The ironic connection between these two beautiful girls is the fact that they were both born on the same day, exactly ten years apart. I am blessed!!!

I must take time, as I did with Deshon, to speak into the lives of my little girls. Tiffanni and Jaylyn, both of you are so very special to me. I am the man who must set the standard in your life for so many things. I understand that it is my responsibility to share with you the proper love so you won't be fooled by imitations. Many unfortunate little girls grow up without knowing the proper love of a father. As a result, little girls tend to search for love from immature boys who end up playing with their emotions. My desire as a father is to have such a blessed relationship with you that any man who doesn't add up to what I have done for you will never count. My purpose is to set the standard for what you should expect from the man that expresses true love for you. Most men do not know how to override their natural sex drive, so they look for weak-minded women to give them what they want without giving anything in return to these women. This sad chain of events leaves women broken and scarred for the rest of their lives. Sometimes, they are so scarred that once they finally give their hearts to the one man that will treat them like they deserve, he cannot get close to them because of the emotional wall that the young lady was forced to build.

As your father, I make a commitment to you to treat you the way God shows me, and in return, I only ask that you give me the opportunity to escort both of you as virgin brides to your husband. I desire to become acquainted with every intricate detail of your lives; even down to the type of man you will look to marry. I believe with all of my heart that if I treat you like dirt, you will look for those qualities in a man. But if I treat you like the future queens that you are, then you are going to look for someone that must do better than me.

It is no coincidence to have two beautiful girls born on the same day. Imagine my surprise learning that your birthstone—in April—is the diamond, and both of you are my diamonds in the rough. Being a diamond in the rough does not diminish your value in any way. I have learned from my studies that diamonds, like most jewels, have to withstand three character-building challenges to gain their true value. I list them as follows: time, heat, and pressure. I also found that a diamond is not a jewel that can easily be dug out of the ground. As a matter of fact, the diamond is formed so deep underground that it takes volcanic activity to push it to a level in the earth so a man can dig for it. Finally, when it is brought to the surface, its value can later be determined by its flawlessness based on the jeweler's ability to properly handle the stone. I believe that it is my job as a father to allow you to go through your process of time, heat, and pressure, which will form you and increase your value. Then I am to dig from around you all the filth that will attempt to suppress your brilliance. Afterwards, I must carefully chip away the tough exterior you were forced to develop in your refining process, revealing your greatest value through my most flawless handiwork.

It feels strange that I'm not talking to you about responsibilities and leadership skills like I did with your brother, but I realize that your makeup is totally different. As a woman, you are relational and you have been trained in that direction since you were a toddler. You are delicate, and there's a mechanism in you that is comforted when you feel protected. More important, you have a strength that kicks in when you recognize the need to be independent, and it is unmatched by any man.

Jaylyn "Skoota Boot" Williams

I have watched you grow into quite an awe-inspiring young lady. I appreciate the way you approach many of your life's challenges with optimism to overcome whatever hand you've been dealt. I have always been proud to have you as part of my life, and I look forward to many more years of watching you grow physically and spiritually. You have so much to give to everyone you meet. You are gifted to exhort people. You have a way of making people feel good about who they are. I like watching you smile, as well as watching you use your creativity to make what could be a dull time exciting. When I pick you up from school, it blesses my heart to receive the hug and kiss on my cheek. I like asking you how your day was because I never get the same answer.

On a more focused note, I see you using the gift God gave you to reach the issues of the heart of God's people. You have a beautiful singing voice, and I believe that to be just a portion of your life's work. It is my belief that you will be a motivational speaker, which will be a culmination of the things that you have been through. I believe that you have been separated for the purpose of God, and He will see to it that you have everything you need to be successful. There is no need for you to search for attention or love from any other source. If you never feel loved from anyone else in your life, know that you have been loved unconditionally   by your mother and me, as well as your family and mine.

I must say that your mother has done a wonderful job of seeing to it that you had everything needed to maintain your life. It is not an easy job to raise a child, but she has succeeded in such a great way. I am honored to see you blossom, and at the same time anxious to see you mature into the woman that God has ordained you to be. Wisdom exudes from your very being. Jaylyn, you can do anything that you put your mind and heart to do.

Tiffanni Erin Gunby

I want to take time to write to Daddy's little midget and mommy's ladybug. I bless you because seeing you being born brought me closer to God. The moment that I held you in my arms, I knew that my life was really about to change. Maybe it was the way you were crying, or maybe it was the fact that the only thing that calmed you was holding my finger to your mouth. I just knew that I was going to have my hands full. I was so excited that for the first two weeks of your life, you slept on my chest. I am so grateful to your mother for having you as an addition to our family.

You are a worshiper. Music moves you. I can relate to some of your worship experiences because I am a musician. I watch you as you enjoy the different flavors of music. Music is cool, but I feel compelled to warn you of the pitfalls of being a worshiper. Sometimes, it is very easy to get caught up in the beat and miss the message. My prayer is that I can help train your ear to follow after the things of God. There are a number of choices that you may make, but remember to focus only on what God desires for you to have.

Through Father's Eyes

Since the first time I held you in my arms, I knew that this day would come; a day that Daddy's Girl would begin to live her life as a young woman. Never have I been so proud of you than I am right now. I never imagined that you would grow so fast, but I had to face the reality of watching you change and become more beautiful every day. Now, you are being propelled toward womanhood, and I wish you could have stayed in my arms forever, but I must allow you room to grow. I made a commitment to love you unconditionally for the rest of your life in hopes of your making a commitment to keep yourself pure until you are married to the man who treats you one hundred times better than I have. To watch you grow has been quite a surprise, although you're becoming a young woman, you're still Daddy's Girl—through your father's eyes.

I Love You with All My Heart,

Daddi (D. Gunby)

6

You Complete Me

As I pondered over the content of this chapter, I was immediately reminded of one of my wife's favorite movies, "Jerry Maguire." There was a scene on the elevator in the movie where a couple who couldn't speak used signed language to share their love for one another. The young lady pointed to the man, then with her two index fingers, formed a circle in the air and then pointed to herself. She expressed to the man in her life one of her precise thoughts in that one moment of passion. She exclaimed, "You complete me."

It is my responsibility to approach my thoughts with extreme caution. My purpose is to totally express my heart specifically to three women who play an intricate role in my life. I would like to thank my mother, Collette L. Gunby; my sister, Kelley M. Thompson; and most important, my wife, Tamar Gunby. These three women are primarily responsible for the man I have become. Society dictates that a woman cannot raise a man, but I am here as a result of the love, care, and passion of three women who wanted to see me succeed.

Dear "Lady"

As far back as my mind allows me to go, I am brought to my knees by the love you have constantly shown. I recall going to work with you at Equifax and meeting all of your coworkers. I didn't totally understand the reason you left such wonderful people to come home and spend time with your family, but I appreciated every moment that you dedicated to us. I never understood why all those people kept coming to the house to listen to Daddy read from the Bible, although I did enjoy listening to them sing. After awhile, I got used to having them over, and made some pretty cool friends who we have known for more than twenty years. I saw strength exude from your very being like the superhero characters I watched on Saturday morning when Dad was in and out of the hospital. You kept everything going so that neither Kelley nor I ever missed a beat. I recall buying the first van for this ministry, which you and Dad started. As a result of the ministry, more people began to come to our home. Sometimes we would pack up the orange Cadillac that Dad affectionately called "Mule" and go to other places and listen to Dad read the Bible to another group of people in a building called a church. Dad would come home excited about speaking at a church, and he soon began talking about getting one. The next thing I knew Dad went and found another place to read from the Bible; this time at a hotel every week. The people didn't fit in our house anymore, so I guess that is why we moved. I enjoyed going to dinner at that restaurant every time Daddy finished reading from the Bible.

As time marched onward, we moved again and again, because each place eventually became too small. I enjoyed every bit of what was going on at that time. It never bothered me that I was there all day, every day. I would get up to go to school and was fortunate enough to see you occasionally.

The next thing I knew, you and Dad had moved us to the entire top level of this complex. I learned that when Dad read from the Bible, it was known as church. Dad finally got the church he was always talking about. The only thing I didn't like about church was that we had to straighten up all seven hundred or more of those chairs that the people messed up after Dad laid his hands on their heads.

I never did thank you for keeping me out of trouble with Dad because I used to talk while he was preaching. Thanks for making the suggestion that I could sit in that special chair behind the drums. I really learned a lot. That is why every time you sent me to the sanctuary to practice my piano lessons; I would come back to the office with tiny beads of sweat on my face. I knew you would understand. As it turned out, I ended up playing the drums for you later in the ministry.

I recall that amazing strength that manifested in you when Dad died. I saw the doctors carry you in the room, but I watched God carry you through the rest of your life. You have been such an inspiration to me, and I believe that no one can give you the credit that you really deserve. I watched you sit down at the closing table to handle a one million dollar deal only months after Dad died. You were so in tune with him that even beyond the grave; your love caused you to see his vision come to pass.

There were times I couldn't focus on school or anything else, and you would stop everything to see to it that Kelley and I were properly taken care of. Most parents would probably try to buy their children's happiness, but not you. The godly mother you were exerted amazing control over the businesswoman you became. There are not many moms like you. Most women in your situation would have gone to find another man to help raise their children, but you knew that God was everything you needed to bring us to our destinies. Amazingly, you still made our house a home, and I'm grateful for who you are. Thank you, Lady. You're the greatest.

K.T. & Lee

You are the sister and brother in love that every brother wished they had. We have been through a number of things individually, as well as together. You are my road dog. Thanks for all those times you let me tag along and enjoy my time with your friends. I did not have a big brother to look out for me, but I had you. Sometimes, I had to look out for you and jack a few people up for you, but together, we got the job done. Our relationship really began to sprout after Dad died because we had a common ground. We have the greatest parents in the whole world. In our lives, we've had a lot of good times, and some of the worst times, but somehow, we made it through. I never knew what you were thinking because you were always in the background and quiet, but I always knew when something was going on with you. I now know that you and Dad had a different relationship when I think back to your getting up at five o'clock in the morning to see him off some days to go to dialysis. I loved Dad too, but I was willing to wait until he got back to talk to him. However, I understand that father-daughter relationship, and I understand the necessity of a father to speak into the life of his little girl.

You grew up and became a woman because of the information that was shared, and through your experience of working in the ministry at a young age. Thanks for being the example of how to maintain a level head in the craziest situations. There is not a brother on this earth that loves his sister more than I love you. You are my ace. As you know, I never had individuals that I could totally trust to share my heart until I got married, but you were there when I needed you, and I appreciate that.

We have come a long way from loading and unloading equipment from the green van. You are an intricate part of the legacy started by our parents. Without you, I probably would not have gotten to this point in my life. Whether you know it or not, I learned so much from you, and I am grateful for the experience of having you as my sister. We must continue to encourage one another, and the next generation, of the goodness of God and all that He has planned for them. We have an obligation to continue the vision.

I watch many preachers on television, and it seems they all have spiritual sons, but I wonder what they are doing with their own children. You and I are fortunate enough to work side by side with our mother as she proclaims the Gospel of Jesus Christ. Not only is she a powerhouse, but also she birthed in us the natural ability to proclaim the things of God with conviction. You are a *bad* girl when it comes to ministering the Word of God. I see glimpses of that strength that I saw in mom as she took over the ministry after Dad's death. You have not even tapped fully into the place that God has destined for you to go. Keep your ears open, and he will direct your every step.

I am speaking to your husband when I say this, "Lee, I appreciate you for taken great care of my sister. I watched you go to great extremes to see to it that her needs, physically and emotionally, were provided. My dad would have been honored that you married his little girl. You have not seen the glory of God revealed until Kelley's full potential is totally released through you." She is the finishing touch to you as the original masterpiece. She has qualities that became suppressed when we lost our father. That is why she found a man so close to the makeup of our father, because those traits are destined to come forward. You are equipped to bring them out. K.T., I love you.

"Momi"

You complete me in ways that no other person can. I have an understanding that I came from my mother. My sister taught me some wonderful life lessons, so in a sense, I came from her. But you, you came from me. Before God placed us in time, he set our paths to cross, and I am elated that they did. I have known you since high school, but I never thought we would end up being joined as man and wife. I always 'thought you were above my caliber, but the reality was that I was living life well below my standard. In order for me to one day wrap my arms around the one woman that originally was birthed from me, I had to change my mindset to receive greater than I was expecting.

It is not hard to love you, but it has taken me some time to learn the process on how to love you. I could easily express my thoughts to my mom and my sister because we have a past. You've presented a challenge to me, because with you I am concentrating on where I am going. I had a past with others including girlfriends, but I have a future with you. You are the confrontation that I have been waiting on my whole life. I now have an understanding, and I am waiting to help you maneuver through all of your past hurts and deepest regrets to bring to the surface your true inner beauty. I also have been waiting to receive help in understanding what a man is supposed to do to properly love his wife and family. You began to answer a number of those types of questions for me without opening your mouth.

I may make some mistakes, but I desire to prove to you that I am willing to stick around and see resolution to those mistakes. I understand that you, like most women, have past hurts that are carried from relationship to relationship waiting on that knight in shining armor to rescue you. I have been placed in your life to rescue you from those bondages, and also show you how to help others be freed from some of the same traps. You have been placed in my life to let me know that I have purpose that goes far beyond the pulpit, yet not far from home.

Being married to you has changed my life. You have become my first ministry. I enjoy watching you smile and seeing you happy, and I also enjoy the challenge of making you smile when your happiness is not apparent. Whether you realize it or not, you are everything that I need. You are my sounding board when I need to bounce around some ideas. You are iron when I need to be sharpened. You are my pillow and blanket when I need rest and comfort. You are the reason that I am a husband and father. You are my balance in those times when work or anything equivalent seems to get more attention than my family. Without you, I would still be playing games with my life, and quite possibly accepting a run-of-the-mill lifestyle.

My desire is that I could help you establish patience to see your brilliant ideas come to fruition. I observed you go through the passing of your mother with a quiet strength. Although I had lost my father, it was very hard to relate to you in your time of need. I paid attention to the many changes that you experienced, but I could not find a way to comfort you. There were no words that I could formulate to ease the pain I knew was present in your heart. Your mother was your world, and without her, I was not sure if you would make it through. I put on the brave face when you came around, but in reality, some days I was that eleven-year-old boy staring at the moon when you approached me. By the grace of God, I saw you slowly rise above that delicate matter of the heart to make sure that your family was okay. I really appreciate you for that. You exuded characteristics of the Proverbs 31 woman as you began to make business with your hands. You are amazing to me. I saw you take care of Deshon's schooling, your mother's illness, pregnancy with Tiff, and being the wife of a traveling preacher. Some days, I don't know how you did it, but incredibly, you succeeded.

I had feelings that I later expressed to you about the incredible pressure I saw you under. Those situations were out of my control. I am not talking about your motherly duties, or loving your mother, or even me. I am referring to the mental strain that had me thinking some days that I was going to be raising the children alone. Again, to my awe, you pulled through. With you, I am not afraid of the unknown, I am anxious to see our life together to the end. You have blessed my life in so many ways, but most importantly, you helped to complete me to be the man that I am. Tamar, I am proud of you, and I am proud that I gave you my name. Through thick and thin, we have come this far, and I am looking forward to whatever we have to face, because I know that we will face it together. I love you.

7

Are You Ready For The Takeover?

My purpose is not to incite a riot that will leave our cities in ruin. The takeover I am referring to is more of a spiritual awakening than a physical uprising. It is an invasion against the Enemy that purposed to destroy our homes and snatch the protective cover away from the lives of our wives and children alike. In order for us to launch such an offensive, we must know what we are set to face. I boldly calculate no fatalities to our troops because our conquest is based on the restoration of the family as a unit. This confrontation will bring life to dead issues which people face in our society through the restoration of men to America's fatherless homes. Men, in these next days, must begin to take a stand and once again lead their families with a fervency based on the original blueprint prior to the fall of man.

The Word of God promises us that man will experience an epidemic sparked by the example of an individual whose sole purpose is to turn the hearts of the fathers to their children and the hearts of the children to their fathers. I am in no way claiming to be that one man who will perform this amazing task. However, I do not think it will be one individual, but the workings of many individuals across the span of generations to come who will help accomplish such a miraculous assignment. I do feel sometimes that I am the one chosen for the job of beginning the healing process for my generation.

SYSTEM FAILURE:
REMEDY FOR A BROKEN SYSTEM

The Heart of The Children

I sense that children have a deep desire to know their origin, but not every child is fortunate enough to have answers to their deepest questions. The obvious question that I think most youth in our society are asking is, "Where do I belong?" These words may never be uttered vocally, but are represented through the actions of young people who are crying out for help only to be overlooked without any adult empathy. Someone has got to speak on behalf of the children in a language that can be understood by all parties involved. In a business transaction, lawyers are called in to arbitrate the terms of the deal. Therefore, I pose   this question, "Aren't our children just as important?"

What I propose to do with this book is to answer the S.O.S. call faintly voiced from our youth with a father's perspective to begin the healing process that must take place. We need a healing in America's homes. Children are simply looking for quality time, which is so significant to define that child's self-worth. I owe it to myself to be more than just a baby's daddy. It is my responsibility to raise my children with love, affection, and discipline when it is necessary. The toughest lesson that I had to learn was that work came a distant second to my family. I would be doing myself an injustice if I became successful in the world, but a failure at home. That is what most men are, public successes, but private failures. We have reached this all-time low because we put more emphasis on being someone important outside the home, and not enough on our importance in the home. Amazingly, we justify this insane plea with the sad excuse that we are trying to provide for our families. In reality, your family does not need a two hundred thousand-dollar or five hundred thousand-dollar home. Those are things we attempt to do to please our own selfish desires. The only thing your wife and children need is you. Let us not indulge ourselves in the twisted scheme of this distorted counterfeit. Men, it is up to you to lead your family back to the original masterpiece, which was designed with you in mind. Fathers, you must return home, no matter how long you have been gone to say to your sons, daughters, and wives, *"Forgive me for not covering you the way that I know I should."* You must take the initiative and really *"be the man"* in the situation concerning your family.

I may have been in error with some of the things I am writing in the pages of this book, but I have learned a great deal from sharing my heart. That is a key to becoming a better man; share your heart with your wife and children. They really can benefit from the information you share with them. Most of us will not allow ourselves to become vulnerable, so we put on the front that says outwardly   everything is okay, but inwardly, we are a broken mess. The heart is such a delicate piece of work that it must be handled properly. If the heart is nourished and protected, it grows and flourishes, but if it is mishandled or abused, it will disintegrate in your hands. I have grown to understand that if I can get my stuff together and be open about my failures, as well as my successes, then my children will have a better opportunity to maintain their lives. Men, your presence is a key to a balanced home. You bring stableness to an insecure environment. Therefore, I stand on the belief that if the man is properly put back in his place, not as a dominator, but as a coordinator, then we can change the face of America's homes in no time.

The Takeover

I believe that in order for a man to return home and take over, he must first experience the takeover. I believe that it is a waste of time for a man to attempt to return home who has not prepared himself for the sacrifices that he must be willing to make. Most men, even those who are in the home, concern themselves with trying to make the occupants of their respective homes happy. In most cases, we attempt to show and prove through actions that we are the men we say we are. Those actions are good, but not always enough. The greatest action a man can take is allowing God to become the Lord and Savior of his life. I am not talking about some spooky, hocus-pocus group. I am talking about establishing a relationship with God (not just some higher power) who promises you His grace that is sufficient, but also His mercy, which is everlasting.

I recall reading in Chapter 2 in the book of Acts about the day of Pentecost (the day that the Holy Spirit presented Himself). The events of this particular passage of Scripture are amazing, but I believe that those events took place because of one specific detail.

> And when the day of Pentecost was fully come,
>
> they were all with one accord in one place.
>
> –Acts 2:1, KJV

If you want to see your family whole again, whether you are in or out of the home, try Jesus. I can only speak from experience when I say, "I was messed up as a husband, father, and as a man." God opened my eyes to show me His love that I only had to duplicate at home to my wife, children, and to myself. I took advantage of the things my relationship with God offers, and my family and I are closer than ever, all in part because I changed to what God desired me to be. All of this happened as a result of my taking time to sit down with my wife and children to get with one accord in one place. Once we got on the same page, and my family recognized that I was willing to do more for them by keeping us together, the tension left my home. You must desire to have peace in your home, and you have to stop running to your secret addiction for relief. Once you, as the man, make this determination, then our sons will leave the streets, our daughters will walk away from the strip clubs, and our wives will want to submit to your leadership. Until then, the decision is totally up to you. Make a choice to change the atmosphere of our society by fixing the problems you left at home.

Prayerfully, as you read further in Acts, Chapter 2, you will find people who spoke different languages found a common language as never before. When you allow God to have His way in your life, you will be empowered to speak to the wife and children you have been out of communication with. Just give it a try. Yes, the world's system has failed us. To effectively confront the failure of the world's system, we must provide the remedy for this broken system. **MEN, YOU ARE THE REMEDY!!!**

From the Author

The content of this book announces a clarion call to all men, fathers, and husbands. Stand up! Listen up! Speak up! Take your rightful place in your home as a servant to those God has given you the responsibility to lead! Make an assertive effort to operate intentionally in the original system given to us by God. It is your position to bring order and restoration to your home, and more importantly, fail the world's system by not letting it continue to fail us. As long as there is breath in your body, there is a chance to mend broken promises…

Pastor D. Gunby

THE VOICE…

www.dgunby.com

About the Author

If destiny ever had its hand on a person's life, it was sure upon that of Douglas Gunby. Born in Atlanta, Georgia, to Ronald & Collette Gunby, Doug's life took a drastic turn when he was only four months old. On June 16, a beautiful Father's Day in 1974, Doug's father was shot three times by his wife's father who was merely defending his home. In an effort to express hidden frustrations, Doug's dad reached for his own pistol but it was too late. Three bullets pierced his back and left him paralyzed in a wheelchair for the remainder of his life. This thirty-second life-changing event happened while Doug lay in the arms of his dad; thankfully, he was not harmed.

It's true that time does heal all wounds. Although Doug's father was bitter, the tragedy left him reflective on how he was living his life up until the shooting. In a moment of surrender, Ronald Gunby dedicated two years of his life to consecrated servitude to God. In 1976, he was directed to start Green Pastures Christian Ministries, Inc. Doug was just two years old when he got his first taste of ministry. Within the next ten years, Doug's knowledge in helping to restore lives began with his own personal experiences.

At thirty-two years old, Doug found his niche in society. His destiny became crystal clear. His passion has become imparting purpose in men. According to Doug, a man's main purpose is to redirect everything that society and others say that they're not, into what they ultimately are supposed to be. Doug found joy in the pain of his past by sharing with others how he overcame the obstacles in his life. Being fatherless at age eleven due to the death of his dad in 1986, addictions to alcohol, drugs, and women are just a few of the hurdles that Doug shares with his audience. He now reaches out to individuals, both young & young at heart in schools, churches, and corporations. This young man is filled with wisdom beyond his years. He is **"The Voice of the Next Generation"**.